My Father, Humming

ALSO BY JONATHAN GILLMAN

Grasslands (short stories)
The Magic Ring (short stories)
The Marriage Test (one-act play)

My Father, Humming

POEMS

Jonathan Gillman

Antrim House
Simsbury, Connecticut

Copyright © 2012 by Jonathan Gillman

Except for short selections reprinted for purposes of
book review, all reproduction rights are reserved.
Requests for permission to replicate should
be addressed to the publisher.

Library of Congress Control Number: 2012951112

ISBN: 978-1-936482-37-5

Printed & bound by United Graphics, Inc.

First Edition, 2013

Book Design by Rennie McQuilkin

Cover Design by Peter Good

Author Photograph by Pam Nomura

Antrim House
860.217.0023
AntrimHouse@comcast.net
www.AntrimHouseBooks.com
21 Goodrich Road, Simsbury, CT 06070

For

my parents,

my wife,

my children

Acknowledgments

Grateful acknowledgment is made to the editors of *Beginnings* (journal of the American Holistic Nurses Association) where the poem "Anniversary" first appeared.

Thanks to the Greater Hartford Arts Council for a Solo Writers Fellowship which helped support completion of the manuscript.

Thanks to Maureen for her encouragement.

And thanks beyond words to Pam, who lived it, talked it, laughed it, cried it—and without whom, nothing.

Author Note

My father was a classically trained pianist, with a certificate from Juilliard, and a nationally known mathematician with a brilliant mind. By the time he died a few years ago, with Alzheimer's, little remained of the person he had been.

The poems in this volume started out not as a "tribute" of any kind, but simply as my way of dealing with what was happening to my father while trying to figure out how to reach him. Touch was one way; music was another. And when he hummed along with me as I played his piano—even though so much else of who he had been was gone—it was clear: not only could he still make music, but, for the first time, he could make it with me.

In the end, I understood that what was happening to him happens to us all. *My Father, Humming* is a tribute to what it means to be a child—a parent—a human being.

Table of Contents

A House with Music in It / 1

I

The Photo on My Piano / 5
My Father Humming / 7
A House with Music in It, II / 8
The Music Box / 10
My Father, Playing / 12
My Father's Millions / 13
Mortality / 15

II

Killing Time / 19
Keys / 21
There Was the Day / 23
Down the Stairs / 24
Love Notes / 26
Memories / 28
My Parents' Hands / 30
Down the Stairs, II / 32
Husband / 35
Down the Stairs, III / 37
At Home / 39
My Father's Millions, II / 41
My Father's Hands / 42
My Father's Millions, III / 44
My Father's Mind / 45
The Hospice Nurse / 46
The Heart of It / 47

The General / 49
Names / 51
One and All / 52
My Father's Way / 54
My Father's Music / 56
The Final Time / 57
Visiting My Father / 58
My Father's Hands, II / 60
Like Death / 61
Anniversary / 62
My Father, Humming, II / 64
The Bones of My Father / 66
My Father, Humming, III / 67
Good Night / 68
Leave Taking / 69
The Tide / 70
My Father's Piano / 72
Appeal / 73
End of a Visit / 74
Final Moment / 75

III

Spring / 79
When Word Comes About My Father / 81
Absence / 83
Requiem / 84
My Father's Voice / 85
Memorial Service / 86
Two Months Later / 87
Final Instructions / 88
End Notes / 89

About the Author / 91

A House with Music in It

You step into the house
and hear the music,
stop, breath held,
push the door shut behind you,
lower the groceries to the floor,
hoping the bag won't crinkle,
and stand, eyes shut,
taken so far from sounds
of the world outside—
as if it doesn't exist.
There is only, in the other room,
piano, player, and the music,
passing through your pores,
penetrating your heart,
lodging there so deep
it's hard to imagine
a time it wasn't there,
or there might come another
when you walk in to nothing,
his hands not on the keys,
no magic in his fingers,
vibration of the twisted strands of metal
gone,
the silence emptier
for what it used to hold.

I

The Photo on My Piano

In the photo on my piano,
my father and I
sitting at his piano,
right hands on the keys,
posing for his mother.
I'm on his lap,
his arms on either side—
my hand a child's,
years to go before
it becomes my own,
his already his,
big enough to span an octave,
and a few more keys besides.

I didn't sit
at a piano again
for years,
a gift he gave
he couldn't have himself.
As soon as the shutter clicked,
he scooped me up,
carried me into the corner,
put me down,
surrounded by
my toys and games,
and while I played,
sat down at his piano
and practiced
over, and over,
muttering and frowning—

from time to time
glancing over,
looking as if he wished
he was there too,
having my childhood
of blocks and trains
instead of his,
filled with arpeggios
and contrapuntals,
mordents left and right.

My Father, Humming

I don't know
how you felt
when you played,
head bent as if
inside the notes.
I do know
you used to hum,
accompanying yourself,
maybe not aware.
One couldn't tell
from listening to you drone
what piece it was,
all tuneless and the same—
immersed so far,
like what they say
about the drowned
becoming one with water.

A House with Music in It, II

I'm twelve,
coming home with friends,
bounding up
onto the porch
in the Indiana
summer afternoon,
crickets and cicadas
making a loud
whirring with their wings,
sweat sticking
to forehead, shirt and neck,
baseball glove
under my arm.
I stop when I hear
the piano from inside,
turn toward my friends,
shake my head,
pull open the door,
shut it behind me
without a click,
step into
the cool dark of the house,
my father at the piano
straight ahead,
humming as he plays,
every now and then
a "Damn it"
as he misses a note.
He doesn't pause,
doesn't look up,

doesn't change his rhythm,
as I tiptoe through,
past the table
covered with
his important work,
the air conditioner
behind it
humming its own tune.
I climb the stairs,
trying to avoid
the ones that creak.
The music—
something of Beethoven,
loud and passionate—
follows me
down the hall
to the door
of my room;
I step inside,
shut it out,
open the windows,
toss my mitt aside,
turn on the radio,
smile a little
at Chuck Berry singing
"Roll over, Beethoven,"
flop down on the bed,
pull out my
toy baseball game,
and go on
being twelve
in nowhere Indiana
on a sticky
summer afternoon.

The Music Box

I'm sitting at my piano,
playing a piece
that's new to me,
one of Bach's English suites,
the Prelude in E minor,
going through it
again and again,
note by note,
trying to find the music in it.
Finally, there's a phrase,
a few strung together,
parts of it becoming mine.
I play more surely,
hearing patterns,
not just a random group
of unrelated notes,
a puzzle being solved.
And then I hear,
in one phrase, and another,
music my father played.
I'm seven.
It's Saturday morning.
He's at the piano
in the living room,
sunlight streaming in.
I'm in my room,
playing on the floor.
I'm not listening,
lost in my toy cars.
It's in the air I breathe,

sticks deep,
seeps back out,
bit by bit, in time.
Years later, I exhale
and there it is,
an invisible
music box
my hands open
and out it pops,
kept closed up all this time—
what he gave so long ago
I never knew till now.

My Father, Playing

They weren't many,
but there were times
deep in the night
when it wasn't for his mother,
or an audience,
or practicing for this or that—
when there was just a light,
the piano and himself,
floating in whatever ether
music lives in.

My Father's Millions

My father's trying
to make his millions,
now, late in life,
as if how he lived before—
not enough.
He's not complete
till he's got his.
"Why?" my mother asks,
"We don't need
more hare-brained schemes."
He's old and slow
and out of touch,
but on he goes
trying to be
what he's never been—
a gung-ho salesman
hawking air ionizers
that sit in boxes
piled high
around his study,
and when turned on
only buzz;
peddling cell phone cards,
four cents a minute;
charts to convert
inches into meters,
miles to kilometers,
as if anybody cares;
and vitamins
to prolong life.

Why shouldn't he
make millions?
He's proof himself—
he takes a dozen
every day
and look at him,
hale and hearty
at eighty-five.

Mortality

My father's trying
to live forever—
he knows it's never
been done before
but he can be the first—
he's looked it up,
he's thought it through,
he has a plan,
he's got it down:
take pills and vials
of vitamins and minerals,
trace elements
and unknown cures,
and add to it
huge dollops of the will—
want anything enough,
why not?

II

Killing Time

Six months after yowling
I was trying to kill him,
talking on the phone
while driving,
and I so angry
I wouldn't talk for months,
my father has
four by-passes.
I visit in the hospital.
There he is,
lying on his back,
eyes shut, mouth open,
a frailer version
of the man
who always had to do
everything himself
till fainting
the week before.
He's not the same,
will never be again—
can't dress himself,
walk fifteen feet,
needs help getting
in and out of bed.
He's changed too
in how he is,
for the first time knows—
vitamins or quackeries,
it'll happen to him too.
He's kinder now,

remembering me young,
how sweet I was
at three, at four, at five,
new stories
every day,
repeated many times,
as if some part
did notice
and forgot, till now.
I sit and watch this man,
so different from before,
and all my anger goes.

Keys

Half asleep
on the couch
in their living room,
I hear my father's voice:
"Look! I found some keys!"
he says,
sounding like a child.
When I get up
ten minutes later
mine are missing.
I look all around—
nowhere to be found.
"What happened to my keys?" I ask.
He stares at me.
"The keys you had—
where'd they go?"
Still no response,
as if suddenly
I'm speaking
some unknown language.
I look again,
ask again.
Still nothing.
"Try his key rack,"
my mother says.
And while he watches
I take my keys
off the rack
where they were

hanging neatly
beside rows of his,
none of them
unlocking
anything anymore.

There Was the Day

There was the day
the days got jumbled—
Monday was Thursday
and Friday Wednesday,
and try as you might
you couldn't remember
which month it was,
as when the wind
picks the leaves up
in a swirl
and puts them down
all scattered.

Down the Stairs

My father's going
downstairs to bed,
my mother helping.
It looks like a disaster
waiting to happen—
tied together by a rope
running from waist to waist—
like the invisible tether
which has bound them for so long
neither can remember
a time before
when they were free
to fall on their own,
not pull the other with them.
She's done this since
the time he took a tumble
and it was hours
before she got him up.
At each step
his foot searches the air
for the one below,
my mother above, waiting;
after he's stood
not moving for a while,
reminding him,
"You're going down the stairs,
the right foot next."
At the landing
there's a chair
he sits on,

shuts his eyes.
She rouses him with
"Only nine more to go,"
puts her arm under his,
tries to lift him.
For a moment it's not clear
if he will make it.
"You have to help me here," she says,
"I can't do this by myself,"
and when he stands,
points him down the stairs,
puts his hand on the railing,
steps back
till the rope
is taut between them,
and on they go.

Love Notes

She comes home
from a morning out,
finds on the kitchen counter
a note in his shaky hand:
"I love you,"
her full name
on the line below,
and, beneath that,
taking up half the page,
his name, signed,
first and last,
as if he was sixteen
wanting to let
the world know
what he'd discovered
and couldn't keep secret.
She finds the same note
all over the house:
on the bathroom counter,
the dining room table,
one beside him in the study
where he sits at the computer.
She comes up behind him,
puts her arms
around his shoulders,
slides her cheek
next to his—
"I love you too,"
saying his name, first and last,
and nuzzling his ear,

smiles as she adds her own,
the one her parents gave her
and the one they've shared
for all these years.
He turns his head toward her.
In his look she sees
he doesn't know
what she's talking about.
She picks the note up
that sits beside him,
kisses it,
holds it in front
for him to see—
still no response,
his face as blank
as the computer screen
he's been staring at.

Memories

We're driving off;
a block from home
my father says,
"Stop. We have to go back.
I forgot something."
"What's that?" I ask,
turning the car around.
"I left my memories."
He's opening the door
before I stop,
trying to step out,
still buckled in.
"Let me," I say,
undoing the belt,
helping him up,
and he is off,
shuffling toward the house.
I'd offer to
go in alone,
but I don't know
what it is
I'm looking for—
what color, size, or shape,
hidden or in plain sight.
"Do you know where?" I ask
when I catch up,
thinking he means
a calendar with dates
or book with photographs.
He doesn't answer,

and while I search
in all the places
I think likely—
counters, drawers,
kitchen, living room, and study—
he makes his way, unaided,
to the music room,
where I come up to him,
take him by the elbow.
"Nothing here," I say,
"We better go,"
while he stands
trying to remember
what he's doing there.

My Parents' Hands

In the night
he makes his way
back to the piano,
sits on the bench in silence,
no one else around,
looks at the music
open before him;
it makes no sense,
its black marks floaters
drifting this way, that;
every time he blinks
more appear
till the air
is filled with them.
He shuts the light off,
sits there in the dark,
fingers fluttering to
a lifetime of
sonatas and concertos
that echo in his head.
His wife beside him
he did not hear come in
leans over,
starts to speak;
he shushes her.
"Bend closer," he wants to say;
"Put your ear next to mine,
and you can hear it too."
Instead, she takes the hand
that joined with hers

years before,
kisses the fingers,
raises it to her face,
holds it against her skin,
blue veins on the back
pulsing against her cheek.

Down the Stairs, II

My father's going
downstairs to bed,
my mother
standing by to help.
They do this
twice a day—
up in the morning,
back down at night.
When he comes up
she walks behind,
ready, if he teeters,
to steady him with a hand,
ease him into
the chair on the landing,
after he rests,
help him back up,
the way she used to
when I was learning,
hands down to catch me—
but I'm miles away,
no use to either.
Going down,
she has a rope,
tied to his belt,
wrapped around her waist.
The plan: if he starts to fall,
she, a pound
for every year alive,
will somehow stop him.
She's too stubborn

to move him upstairs,
won't give up
the way they've lived
for all these years.
Instead, each day
after dinner
she holds his hand,
kisses his cheek,
says, "Okay, it's time,"
fastens the rope
to each of them,
grits her teeth
and off they go—
forgetting her own mother,
how she lay
half the night
at the bottom of the stairs,
calling for
her sleeping husband—
not thinking,
though my father's shrunk
he's still ten inches taller,
outweighs her
forty pounds—
once he starts to go,
no matter how strong her will,
both would end up
in a jumble on the floor,
hoping nothing's broken—
not laughing

at how foolish,
not guffawing
at how limbs
like chicken parts
are sprawled across the landing—
but lying there,
seeing if she's hurt,
trying to untangle
one from the other,
get back up,
help him up too—
or wait for hours
till a friend happens by
and finds them both
still there.

Husband

Alone in the night
the two of you, back then,
your hands at ease on her,
knowing
what notes to hit,
both high and low,
that made her rumble
deep and full—
at times, slow and gentle,
at others
fast and furious,
or light and breathless,
building toward crescendo,
and after,
the calm that followed,
till finally stillness,
nothing but ripples
still vibrating
in her, in you.

Now your hands
don't make
the same sweet sounds,
nothing as
it used to be—
no tune or harmony.
You know she'd rather
stay here, quiet,
hoping you don't try.
Instead you sit in silence,

the two of you together,
close but still,
hands resting
lightly on her,
smiling as you remember
the way you made her sing.

Down the Stairs, III

It happens every night:
my mother
following my father
down the stairs,
not accepting help.
"I'd get used to it," she says,
"and then when you're not here..."
Today too
tied together
by a rope
that runs from waist to waist,
and when they reach the bottom
her reward—
after she
changes his diaper,
cleans him up,
puts on his pajamas,
tucks him into bed
and he sleeps there,
sixteen hours—
to do it again
in the morning,
till the time,
his energy used up,
he collapses,
slides out of the chair,
lies there on the landing,
a turtle on its back.
Nothing she does
can make him move;

she has to call 9-1-1,
have the firemen,
robust young men,
carry him upstairs.
After that
he doesn't seem to notice
that where she leads him
doesn't involve ropes,
the invisible tether
as strong as ever,
guiding him to a bed
he won't get up from.

At Home

The fireman, standing
on the landing
in their home
in Austin, Texas,
towers over my father
lying on his back,
looks down and asks,
"Where are you, sir?"
My father answers,
"New York City,"
and laughs.
The fireman repeats,
a little louder,
"Do you know
where you are, sir?"
My father answers,
a little louder,
"Yes, New York City,"
and laughs,
a little louder.
My mother
smiles at the fireman,
"He does this sometimes,"
says to my father,
"You know where we are,
at home, in Austin"—
while he keeps
staring up past both,
and smiling,
as if at a memory

of him, a boy,
lying on the sidewalk
looking up at
the tall buildings
of New York City.

My Father's Millions, II

Less than a month
after spending
three days in seminars
in motel meeting rooms
in Amarillo,
and returning
Motivated for Success,
as far from his
short-sleeved shirts
with bow ties
and pocket protectors
as wearing jump suits
covered in spangles
or playing rock and roll,
my father has
a quadruple by-pass.
He's never the same,
no longer able to do
almost anything himself—
for all we know
still selling in his mind
to people everywhere.
My mother has to clear out
stacks of merchandise
clogging up
the house's arteries
so there is room
to get a hospital bed
into his study,
a place for him to spend
his final days
dreaming of Success.

My Father's Hands

My father's hands are peasant hands—
short, thick, squat, wide—
hands that served his father well,
working in fields,
picking grapes,
or in warehouses,
stacking crates,
the only music
what a man could make
humming while he worked.

His mother wanted more,
for him to do
what she could not
because of him—
when he was still a child
sat him on a phone book,
feet dangling off the floor,
set before him
music of the cultured classes,
commanded: "Learn it, play it,
make us be like them;
play," she urged, "play more,"
and frowned:
"I wish you had my hands."
If she could, she would have
broken all his fingers,
re-set them, every one,
long, delicate, graceful, sensitive,

nothing of his father's
in any one.

No matter how well done,
what the accolades,
still she commanded,
"Reach, reach farther"—
no matter how
they tried to stretch,
nothing but his father's
piano mover hands.

Even after she was gone,
every time he played
he heard her commands,
till, years later,
his aging hands—
the fingers thin and bony—
lie resting on his chest,
twittering from time to time
to what he hears inside,
every note
exactly as it
is meant to be,
no one to say otherwise.

My Father's Millions, III

My father,
no longer getting
out of bed,
lies, eyes open,
pointing at the wall,
saying to my mother
when she comes in,
"I'm writing a textbook
for college students.
It's all there
on the wall,
it's going to be
a big success.
All I need
is paper, pen
and typewriter."
My mother responds,
"That's great—
I'll bring them
first thing in the morning";
and he keeps lying there,
staring at the wall
and smiling.

My Father's Mind

All that
and your mind went too,
your pride and joy
that you lorded it over
everyone with,
correcting
how people spoke,
even your wife,
as if English was logical
and she wasn't smart enough
to get it right.
See where you ended up:
this woman you put down
and never thought your equal
is now the one
taking care of you,
and when what you say
makes no sense,
she doesn't
correct your grammar,
fill in what you left out,
grill you on what
you really meant.
She holds your hand,
kisses your cheek,
tells you she loves you,
glad you're still alive.

The Hospice Nurse

It's our husband, father,
we who at the funeral
will sit front and center,
but she's the one
who tends him now,
feeds him, bathes him, dresses him,
changing shirt, pants and diaper,
who sees the signs,
"Do not resuscitate,"
"Do not call 9-1-1,"
her charge, to keep him living,
but no heroics.
And when he dies,
her reward
another assignment
that won't last long.
Will anyone remember
to invite her to the service?
Who will comfort her
for what she's lost,
the second in a year,
her hands knowing him,
his bony hips and ribs,
better than her boyfriend's body
or her own,
knowing nothing else—
who he was before,
how he got here,
only that
this is where he is
and she's the one
that's needed now.

The Heart of It

I'm at the piano
in my father's music room
playing a piece by Bach,
part of the Partita
in G major;
he lies in his bed
in the room adjacent,
asleep, no doubt,
a little weaker
every day,
his system steadied by
a metronome
that helps it keep
the proper time.
At one phrase,
every time it comes around
I hear it
as he played it,
on this piano
years before,
as if it's been
there inside
all this time.
I don't see either of us—
me, a child,
he a young man then,
any more than
I see him now,
lying there,
mouth open,
half alive.

I only hear the music,
each string that's struck—
the heart of it
still vibrating.

The General

You lie there
like a cadaver
in an ancient picture,
with bony face and hand.
Are you the person
who got so upset
when you thought
someone slighted you—
ready to fight duels,
go to war for
imagined insults?
Where are they now,
your principles
you would have killed
ten thousand for?
Do you remember
what you were so
incensed about,
what affront
you could not ignore?
Do you even know
who you are,
where you are,
what your name is?
who this is
who strokes your forehead,
kisses your cheek,
says she loves you?
Is it someone hired
or the woman

you shared your life with?
If you had it to do over,
knowing it would come to this,
would you be kinder, gentler—
or are you, even now,
legs twitching, lips moving,
giving marching orders,
fighting battles
you think matter,
while the one
you can't defeat
attacks your
unprotected flank.

Names

The person is right there;
I know who he is,
where he lives,
what he does,
how I'm connected to him,
but his name escapes me,
a note I wrote myself
I cannot find.
Sometimes, hours later,
looking for something else,
there it is.
Sometimes it doesn't
come back at all,
a blank,
till someone says it,
and I think, "Oh, yeah, of course"—
and I wonder:
Is that what happened to you?
Is this how it began?

One and All

After reading Villon

For a long while
death kept its distance—
all four grandparents
into my twenties,
both parents
well past eighty—
content to watch and wait,
take someone else instead.
It may come early,
it may come late,
but it comes,
one and all.

Then it got the grandparents
one by one;
an aunt, so full of it
they sewed her up
and sent her home;
one uncle of a stroke;
the other starved himself;
my sister found a lump,
caught it early,
still around, for now;
my father can't do
anything himself,
not much longer for this world.
It may come early,
it may come late,

but it comes,
one and all.

I used to think
stay active, fit,
I could go on and on,
but lately I've been
tired, sluggish,
know it has its eye on me.
It may come early,
it may come late,
but it comes,
one and all.

My Father's Way

I'm angry with you.
I can't go in
and say good night,
not and mean it.
I'm upset at a story
my mother told
of taking you to a concert
the year before,
and, because the musicians
played not the way
you thought they should,
you booed,
and when you wouldn't stop,
she took you home.
You believe, she adds,
they should have played
the way Beethoven intended.
And what is that, I wonder,
standing at the door,
looking at you sleeping.
Did Beethoven
tell you himself?
It's been hours
and I'm still angry
at what this brings back up:
how you imposed
your one right way
on everything we did.
I take a breath,
nod good night,

turn to go,
to play the piano,
not out of meanness,
a torture you can't escape,
which not that long ago
you would have run
screaming from—
"That's not how
it's supposed to be played!"
I don't pretend it is.
But this way's mine,
this long and slow—
finding my own music
in the notes
the Maestro wrote.

My Father's Music

My mother puts a CD on.
It's you playing,
your friend on cello;
the music's spirited,
with all the emotion
Beethoven's famous for.
On your bed,
your breathing doesn't change—
mouth open,
head to one side,
hand on your chest,
the cover up and down.
What do you hear?
Do you recognize the piece,
know it's you?
Do you remember playing it?
And when you did,
did you imagine
it would come to this?
Do you still hear the music?
Or has that gone too,
and all it is—
white noise,
the fog of forgetting
drifting in,
obscuring everything?

The Final Time

There is no journal entry.
No one marked the days
to say, last time
you walked by yourself,
dressed yourself,
drove, ate steak,
played the piano,
or any of
so many things,
though there's an album
full of baby you:
first tooth, first crawl,
first word, first step,
first sitting
at the piano,
first time you drove.
What's clear:
you did these once
and now you don't.

Visiting My Father

I go into my father's room,
lay my hand on his.
"Hi, sweetie," he says,
eyes shut, voice strong.
It's a surprise,
a green sprig in the desert;
he hasn't spoken in days.
"No," I say,
thinking he means my mother—
he never calls me that.
"She's in the other room.
This is your son."
And though I stay there
hand on his
twenty minutes longer,
he says nothing more,
but goes on sleeping,
or whatever it is he does,
eyes shut, to pass his days.

And then,
the person who never
opens his eyes,
while I am standing there
holding his hand,
opens them, wide,
looks right at me,
as if he knows me
and is surprised, or glad.
"Remember me," I say,
"I'm your son,"

saying the nickname
only he calls me.
His mouth opens part way,
as if he's going to speak,
or smile, or both—
then nothing—
it stays open,
opens wider.
His eyes close,
his mouth follows,
his breathing settles in.

Later
he opens his eyes
even wider
and stares at me,
says in answer
to my question,
"Yes, I'm warm enough—
Don't squeeze my hand too tight."
And then,
with my hand
still squeezing his,
but not so tight,
he brings his other over,
fingers thin and bony—
paws at the air with it
until it finds
what it is looking for
and settles down on mine.

My Father's Hands, II

My father's hands
are not as they used to be.
They have not moved
to written music
in years,
but lie on his chest,
or on the bed beside him,
twitching to a CD
of a piece he used to play.
If, while he slept,
they could make their way
back to the keyboard,
they'd find the notes
his memory has lost.
Instead, I'm the one
remembering
hearing it as a child
before I slept—
I'm the one sitting
barefoot at his piano,
bringing my fingers down,
making the music
which hangs here in the air,
drifts up to his bed,
penetrates his dreams,
moving from
his hands to mine
and back again.

Like Death

After Villon

Like death warmed over
or a corpse not cold,
one the crows and maggots
haven't got to yet,
you lie there
all skin and bone,
clinging as to the ledge
of a tall building.
You can't sit, can't stand, can't walk,
can't dress yourself,
can't pick up food,
can't put it in your mouth,
still chew
but forget to swallow,
can't wipe yourself,
can't even shit on the pot,
wrapped in a diaper
like an infant—
can't see, can't talk,
not and make any sense,
can't remember diddley.
But your heart still beats.
You call this living?

Anniversary

She goes into the room,
sits beside the bed,
takes his hand.
"You know what today is?"
she asks the body
that does not respond.
"Our anniversary.
It's a big one—seventy."
She stops, remembering
the year before,
going out,
he in his chair,
complaining about the food—
he couldn't have been
too badly off—
lifting him into it,
out of it,
how hard that was,
how much he had declined,
no inkling then—
she puts it out of mind.
"Some of them
were difficult—
you weren't always
the easiest.
But for better or for worse—"
And she thinks, but does not say:
"Squeeze once if you can hear me,
a second time
if you still love me"—
too much to ask,
not daring to hope

or be disappointed;
better to live with memory—
lapsing into silence,
following her thoughts;
and then,
when lost in them,
feeling pressure
on her fingers,
a second time as well.
She squeezes back,
once, twice, and waits—
nothing more,
on his face, no change,
eyes shut, as always.
And as the day
settles into night,
longest of the year,
she stays, hands joined with his,
in silence,
while the room gets dark
so slowly, as if
the light is being
exhaled out,
till all she sees—
a shadow where the window is,
outline of his body
on the bed,
the only sounds
their breathing,
rising, falling,
and so faint
she almost cannot hear
but knows it still is there,
the beating of their hearts.

My Father, Humming, II

I'm at my father's piano,
playing a piece
he used to play,
but not the way
he played it,
not, he's sure, the way
Herr Beethoven intended.
He's hearing it,
not sleeping as he often is,
and he's not happy with it.
Before, he would have
yelled out "Stop!"
or booed, or yowled,
"You're trying to kill me!"
He's not saying much these days.
Before I've played five notes,
he's choking, loud and drastic.
Stop now, I think,
call 9-1-1,
then rush up,
see what I can do.
The caretaker is there—
she's raised the bed,
he's sitting upright,
nothing else to do,
let him work it through.
I keep playing.
The choking gets
louder, more alarming,
a rattle in the throat,
as if this is the end.

My stomach tightens,
but I don't stop—
and this goes on a while,
duet for a son
playing on his father's piano
while his father
gasps his last.
But then the choking lets up,
gets quieter,
changes to a cough,
more like the clearing of a throat,
and stops.
He's still,
and I'm still playing.
I take a breath, relax;
as I go on, I hear,
so faint at first
I'm not sure what I'm hearing:
mmm mmmm, mmm mmmm—
he's humming, tunelessly,
along with me,
the way he used to
when he was playing.
It gets stronger, surer;
there's no mistaking it—
and we go on like this,
the two of us,
making music,
until the piece is done.

The Bones of My Father

He sleeps on the hospital bed,
one end raised—
he's almost upright,
sliding slowly down.
Once an hour
the caretaker grunts,
pulling him back up.
On and on he sleeps,
breathing steady,
not much left of him.
If he doesn't
wake for longer,
take more in,
soon nothing will remain
but bone.
In the morning
I'll pull back the sheets,
discover a cadaver,
still breathing.
And when my mother
kisses the eye socket
with all the love
of seventy years
and says, "Sometimes I think
we're living too long,
don't you?"
the skull will move
from side to side.

My Father, Humming, III

The gift my father gave:
music known in utero,
not heard, but felt,
before the ears were formed,
movement of the fluid
that's in us and surrounds us,
comforts us and calms us,
that place
we do not want to leave
that's mother, father, all.
The slow and quiet way
I play, the edge between
stillness and vibration,
the ripple of the liquid
that is our home
before we see the light.
Now—
so close to letting go
of body, bone and breath,
and going back
to what was there before—
as if reminded of a tune
so far away
he half remembers—
he hears it in my playing.
It echoes through his being
and he begins to hum.

Good Night

I go in to wish him
a quick good night,
hold his hand,
say my name.
I've stayed away all day,
annoyed at this or that,
the things he did
years ago,
the way he was back then,
as if anything
could change that now.
There he lies,
eyes shut, mouth open, face gaunt,
the picture of a corpse.
But he breathes,
mutters something,
breathes again,
and I think:
how do you stay
angry at a baby?
I let go of everything—
squeeze his hand,
kiss his cheek,
whisper, "Good night,"
turn and walk away.

Leave Taking

You've buried both your parents,
your mother, like this,
slowly in a home;
brother, younger than you,
choosing to starve;
so many dear close friends.
You've loved to have him
for so long,
but you have said good-bye
to the person he once was,
the one you shared so much with.
By now, words gone,
laughter, memory,
as far as you can tell,
unless, like a bird
trapped in a house,
he's in there still,
wings banging
against the panes.
Open all the doors,
the windows,
leave them wide,
he goes on flapping
trying to get out.

The Tide

You're strapped here to the bed,
hand-wide strips
crisscrossing your chest,
an X above your heart,
tied snug behind the frame
to hold you upright,
keep you from sliding down,
flopping to one side
while the caretaker feeds you,
spoons your medication in.
We sit here at your feet,
seeing you as if
fastened to
the piling of a dock
near the mouth of
a large river,
no waves,
just the steady
rising of dark water
as the tide comes in—
up to your chest,
your armpits,
covering your shoulders,
up your neck.
This time
when it reaches your mouth
will you clamp shut,
breathe through your nose?
Or will you shut your eyes,
open wide?

Or will it only
reach your chin,
start to recede,
make us wait for
another time,
a higher tide?

My Father's Piano

On my father's piano
the final note
lasts and lasts;
you think it would have faded,
it would be still by now—
but there it is,
going on and on.

Appeal

I am a man
like any other.
I take my pants off
one leg at a time.
And when I reach
my father's state,
beyond the age
of taking care,
in all humbleness,
I say to you:
I know I never
accepted help before;
I need it now
to get me through
these last few hours.

End of a Visit

I go in to say good-bye.
This visit's over.
I take his hand.
I don't know
when I'll be back,
how much longer
he'll be around,
a little weaker
every week,
but even for the weakest,
sometimes it takes
so long to die.

Final Moment

When it comes,
after all this time,
it will be quiet—
not announcing itself
with banners and trumpets.
It'll be in the night
or early morning hours,
no sound, no yell or curse,
nothing that you,
sleeping there beside him,
because you know
the end is near,
will hear.
It will not wake you
or disturb you.
When you do
open your eyes,
what you notice first:
an absence,
no coughing,
or the sound of breathing
interrupted,
nothing but your breath
held a moment,
your heart, beating faster,
thumping in your ears;
on the bed next to you,
his forehead no longer
warm to your touch;
chest no longer

rising, falling—
still;
hands that when you
went to bed
lay on the covers,
sheet clutched in one,
at rest.
You'll put your hands
over his,
move the sheet
that he knocked off
in the night,
cover his left foot,
and leave him lying
almost as he was.

III

Spring

The change isn't much,
you barely notice—
only warmer
a few degrees.
Then you realize:
the grass is getting green;
maples budding red;
willows a different
color pale;
frost long out of the ground;
peepers, like the water, bubbling;
river swollen, full,
about to overflow;
robins hopping;
night crawlers,
after a rain,
all over the pavement;
it's light hours later,
and you feel lighter too.

The change isn't much,
you barely notice,
and then you realize:
the sheet's not
rising, falling
across his chest.
You catch your breath and listen.
The silence seems so deep
nothing could end it.
The white lilies,

fragrant by the bed,
their smell and blossoms fading.
Outside, spring is here,
but in here,
set the thermostat
at eighty-five,
it still won't keep
his face from getting cold.

When Word Comes About My Father

As if I'm on the board
going back and forth
across the salt pond,
intent on
water, wind and sail,
I look up to find
everything gone,
nothing but
the white of fog
that has crept in
without my noticing,
no land or landmarks
anywhere;
I cannot see the place
I just came from,
the sky or green of trees,
cannot see the flagpole
or sand along the shore
though they were there
moments before.
I stand in the middle
looking each direction,
no way to know
which way is what,
where the beach I launched from,
the near end with the houses,
the other side,
the open end
where the water
goes on for miles—

it could be this
or that or that.
If I set off
I might go on and on
and never reach the shore.
After standing for a while,
knowing nothing more,
I pull the sail up,
turn it in
against the wind
and, trusting to my hands,
my arms and legs,
set off,
the surface rippling
beneath the board,
the breeze across my face—
go on like this
what seems like hours
till land emerges,
the skeg scrapes bottom,
and there I am,
inches from where
I started.

Absence

He's not here today,
will not be tomorrow;
there is no longer the chance
he might snap out of it,
even for a moment,
open his eyes,
see me and talk,
the way he used to;
there is
no hand to hold,
forehead to smooth,
cheek to kiss,
no body there—
the room empty,
bed gone
where life used to be,
only memories
locked away inside,
who he was
no longer changing.

Requiem

In my father's music room,
his music on his desk,
his glasses next to it,
as if he took them off
a moment ago
and in another
will put them on again;
in the room above,
where he slept so long,
the bed already gone.
From his piano
the opening notes
of "Moonlight"
hang near the ceiling,
against the walls,
penetrating
wood and stone,
so strong,
a stranger walking in
would feel them and stop,
unable to go on—
vibrations of
the metal strings
reverberating
lower and lower
till they have reached a place
ear can't hear
but heart still knows.

My Father's Voice

At the memorial service,
they played a recording
of my father playing
the Capriccio
of Bach's second Partita,
and I was fine with that,
but when they played
the "Elements" song
and I heard his voice,
strong and sure,
the way I knew it
all my life,
not the feeble tentative
of the last few years,
that was harder,
as if he hadn't
decayed, deteriorated, or died,
but still alive—
there he was
in that box there—
I heard him,
same as ever.
You just have to know
what button to push,
and he comes back to life.

Memorial Service

At the memorial service
it's my father
they're talking about—
his name that's said
over and over—
but it's me I'm hearing,
as if I'm the one
being buried here,
no one else left
between me and the void.
I'm next,
there's no escaping it.

And after I have spoken
and it is done,
it's my two sons
who come up to me
and, without a word,
first one and then the other
hug and hug,
until I know
they know
about the death of fathers—
mine, and theirs,
their children's too—
saying to me now
what they won't be able to
when our turns come.

Two Months Later

It's two months later.
I'm sitting barefoot
on an island,
the ocean forty feet away,
going in and out,
out and in,
the water
we all come from,
go back into
at the end,
the waves, the surf
my father did not like,
stayed away from
all his life.
I turn and watch it
along the shore,
like the piano
at the end of
the first movement
of Beethoven's "Moonlight,"
running in,
running out,
running in again
and lingering,
as it recedes,
all that's left
a curving line of twigs,
seaweed and shells,
the last drops and bubbles
disappearing
as if absorbed
into the sand.

Final Instructions

When I die, don't bury me,
but burn me down
till all that's left is dust.
Set aside a handful,
to mix with yours
when you have moved on too;
and of the rest,
take me to the water
where I have played and splashed and laughed,
go out on it
till all you see is blue and green.
Commend me to the wind
which holds the spirit,
and as you feel it touch your face,
toss this little that remains
gently up into it
to carry where it will,
and be content,
knowing I'm at peace.

End Notes

I sit down at
my father's piano.
The first slow notes
of Beethoven's "Moonlight"
echo in the room
till the air's alive with them,
striking to the bottom of the heart
and lower,
down to the core.

Here, in this room,
through these keys, these notes,
these fingers and this heart,
what he gave me
years ago
I now give back to him;
and if I listen
as I play,
I still can hear
his spirit humming
loud and clear.

About the Author

Jonathan Gillman is the head of the Theater Department at the Greater Hartford Academy of the Arts, a public magnet high school, and the Director of Looking In Theatre, a "teen interactive social issue" theater group. In addition to poetry, he writes fiction, non-fiction, plays and children's stories.

This book is set in Garamond Premier Pro, which had its genesis in 1988 when type-designer Robert Slimbach visited the Plantin-Moretus Museum in Antwerp, Belgium, to study its collection of Claude Garamond's metal punches and typefaces. During the mid-fifteen hundreds, Garamond—a Parisian punch-cutter—produced a refined array of book types that combined an unprecedented degree of balance and elegance, for centuries standing as the pinnacle of beauty and practicality in type-founding. Slimbach has created an entirely new interpretation based on Garamond's designs and on comparable italics cut by Robert Granjon, Garamond's contemporary.

To order additional copies of this book
or other Antrim House titles, contact the publisher at

Antrim House
21 Goodrich Rd., Simsbury, CT 06070
860.217.0023, AntrimHouse@comcast.net
or the house website (www.AntrimHouseBooks.com).

You may also want to visit www.myfatherhumming.com
to post a comment or find additional information.

At www.antrimhousebooks.com
in addition to information on books
you will find sample poems, upcoming events,
and a "seminar room" featuring supplemental biography,
notes, images, poems, reviews, and
writing suggestions.